NEW YORK REVIEW BOOKS

POETS

AMIT CHAUDHURI is a novelist, essayist, poet, and musician. A fellow of the Royal Society of Literature, he lives in Calcutta and the United Kingdom. He has written eight novels, the latest of which is *Sojourn*. Among his other works are three books of essays, the most recent of which is *The Origins of Dislike*; a study of D. H. Lawrence's poetry; a book of short stories, *Real Time*; two works of nonfiction, including *Finding the Raga* (New York Review Books, 2021); and four volumes of poetry. Formerly a professor of contemporary literature at the University of East Anglia, Chaudhuri is now a professor of creative writing and the director of the Centre for the Creative and the Critical at Ashoka University, as well as the editor of literaryactivism.com. He has made several recordings of Indian classical and experimental music, and has been awarded the Commonwealth Writers' Prize, the Los Angeles Times Book Prize for Fiction, the Indian government's Sahitya Akademi Award, and the James Tait Black Prize.

T0038451

Amit Chaudhuri

Sweet Shop
New and Selected Poems
1985–2023

NYRB/POETS

 NEW YORK REVIEW BOOKS   *New York*

THIS IS A NEW YORK REVIEW BOOK
PUBLISHED BY THE NEW YORK REVIEW OF BOOKS
207 East 32nd Street, New York, NY 10016
www.nyrb.com

Library of Congress Cataloging-in-Publication Data
Names: Chaudhuri, Amit, 1962– author.
Title: New and selected poems / by Amit Chaudhuri.
Description: New York: New York Review Books, [2022] | Series:
  New York Review Books poets | Identifiers: LCCN 2022022407 (print) |
  LCCN 2022022408 (ebook) | ISBN 9781681377001 (paperback) |
  ISBN 9781681377018 (ebook)
Subjects: LCGFT: Poetry.
Classification: LCC PR9499.3.C4678 N47 2022 (print) |
  LCC PR9499.3.C4678 (ebook) | DDC 821/.914—dc23/eng/20220520
LC record available at https://lccn.loc.gov/2022022407
LC ebook record available at https://lccn.loc.gov/2022022408

ISBN 978-1-68137-700-1
Available as an electronic book; 978-1-68137-701-8

Cover and book design by Emily Singer

Printed in the United States of America on acid-free paper.
10 9 8 7 6 5 4 3 2 1

Contents

Author's Note xi

SWEET SHOP

Sweet Shop 3

Nakur 4

Just As 5

Shyamalda 6

Petha 7

To My Editor 8

Refugees 10

Spectacles 12

Creek Row 13

Tarting Up 14

The Left 15

Bhim Nag 16

Embrace This Sadness 18

Fingers 19

Love 20

Chhana 21

Can You Tell Me 22

Terror (after Rustom's) 23

Faltu 24

Adil 25

Seeing (in) the Dark 27

Keystone 27

Kalbaisakhi 29

The Killer Punch 30

Ma 31

Sandesh 32

Tapas 33

Tele bhaja 34

Notes in Mid-Air 36

The Garden Path 38

Sadness-Joy 39

FROM **RAMANUJAN**

From Nakhoda Masjid 43

Ramanujan 44

Cambridge 45

Salt and Vinegar 48

Cathedral 49

God 51

Oxford 53

The Fake and the Organic 54

Hamburger 55

Tunnel   57

Reading *Kaddish*   58

Zombies   60

Keith Jarrett   62

Reading Li Shangyin on Emirates While Listening
    to Joni Mitchell   63

Yesterday   64

Radha, Before Term   65

Block C   66

Vinyl   67

The Pleistocene Epoch   68

The Reader   70

Onward Motion   71

Buskers   72

Parents   74

Chalta   75

Tuchchho Kobita   76

Daybreak 1st January   77

Eating at Home   78

Mother   80

Post-Midnight, Rain   81

Apartment   82

Sandesh Mould   83

Orange Juice Concentrate   84

They   85

To a Poem   86

Death-Song   87

Dhak   88

Life-line   89

Our Parents   90

Short Q and A   91

FROM ST CYRIL ROAD AND OTHER POEMS

The Village   121

St Cyril Road, Bombay   123

The Bandra Medical Store   125

St Cyril Road Sequence   127

Letter from the Hills   132

Afternoon Raag   134

Kitchen   137

September   138

Nissim Ezekiel   139

Morola Fry   140

How Do You Fight This Monster?   141

UNCOLLECTED POEMS

The Writers   145

Balthazar   146

Recovery   147

Amazing Sleeplessness   148

Forgotten Poems   150

Chhena Sandesh Bhubaneshwar   151

Cold Soup   152

Clothes-drying   153

TRANSLATIONS FROM BENGALI

Seven Songs by Rabindranath Tagore   157

Dream (Rabindranath Tagore)   162

Banalata Sen (Jibanananda Das)   164

Notes   165

AUTHOR'S NOTE

I FEEL I owe the reader an explanation about the sequence of these selections, which neither move from newest to oldest or the other way round. At the start, the reader will encounter *Sweet Shop* (reproduced here in full, as it was a brief collection). It came out in India (Penguin Random House) and the UK (Salt) in 2019. Going farther in, the reader will move forward in time to selections from *Ramanujan* (Shearsman, UK, 2021). These include poems I wrote after *Sweet Shop* and a prose sequence called "Short Q and A," which I put together at the same time. Then the reader will find themselves sent back, to poems from *St Cyril Road and Other Poems* (Penguin India, 2005), whose earliest poem, the eponymous "St Cyril Road," was written in 1985 and published in the *London Review of Books* in 1986. After this comes a section containing new poems, and an uncollected one, "The Writers," which was published in *The Observer* and now finally finds a home. In the final section are translations I have done over the last decade—seven songs and a poem by Tagore, and one (done very recently) by Jibanananda Das.

I justify the unusual back and forth in time in this way:

Sweet Shop constitutes, in effect, my return to poetry after more than a decade, and is, in fact, a fresh beginning for me as a poet. The poems came to me after I went to North Calcutta in 2018 to take photos of the portraits of founders that hang from the walls of Calcutta's sweet shops (this expedition was related to a bizarre art project I won't dwell on here). So I want the reader to encounter me (as a poet) here first; then move to the poems I wrote later, in the more recent past (*Ramanujan*); catch a glimpse of where I began (*St Cyril Road and Other Poems*); and end with where I am at present.

A word on the early poems. With "St Cyril Road," Karl Miller, the founder and editor of the *London Review of Books*, felt I had moved from being an apprentice to a poet. Something indeed had happened. A shift occurred after I returned to India, to Bombay, on a holiday from London (where I was an undergraduate) in 1985, to visit my parents in the flat they had moved to after my father's retirement. Something about the location (Bandra, a largely Christian area) and the flat (which was on the third storey, in contrast to the twenty-fifth-storey flat we had occupied before my father's retirement) brought out in me the kind of writer I'd become, and emboldened me to write a series of poems about an actual location. Soon after, I started writing a novel and gradually wrote fewer poems, or none for large stretches of time. As a writer, I think I've been less interested in narrative than in making, creation, coming-into-existence. The Calcutta sweet shop allowed me to return to this interest through poetry.

—*Amit Chaudhuri*

Sweet Shop

Sweet Shop

The whole universe is here.
Every colour, a few
on the verge of being barely tolerable.
Every shape as well as minute flourishes
created in the prehistory
of each sandesh by precise pinches.
The horizontal trays
brim (but don't tremble) with mass and form.
The serrations are near-invisible.
You'd miss them if they were deeper or clearer.
The soft oblongs and the minuscule, hard
pillow-shaped ones are generated
so neatly that instinct alone
could have given them shape, and no mould.
In the harmony shielded by the glass
is an unnoticed balance of gravity and play.

Nakur

Nakur!
I knew you by name.
You didn't even populate
my background traffic in allusions.
I wasn't aware I was aware of you
till that afternoon, when you were half a mile away.

I didn't know if you were a sweet or a shop
or a name
or a word in Bangla.
But when I turned left to the lane and you were there
I greeted you over-familiarly.
Past the entrance through which only
staff enter I saw a sanctum,
a temple-space, high on whose walls
hung no secular photograph
but mortal or mythic divinities.
But in the front where a group milled
was pure box-office—an ancient grille
through whose one square gap an arm
retrieved notes and boxes changed hands.
Is it your sandesh that
has pullulations, like a face
that's broken out in fever, or did I
imagine that? Others bought;
I, a flunkey on the pavement, stood
on the margin taking photos on my phone
of you, the grille, the tube-lit shade,
and the crowd. I did not eat
or taste you, but entirely
consumed you and your customers.

Just As

Just as jewellery,
moist cells shining,
or scented erasers you cradled at five,
each carrying
an elephant or tree
or dog, are too delectable
to be spent on their own purpose,
but ask to be eaten,
so sandesh
in its untouchable
heterogeneity
is displayed behind the pane
as in a museum
to be stared at and historicised.

Shyamalda

Shyamalda—
you had possibly travelled
over a thousand miles
when, once,
on our way to Rishra,
pierced by hunger, you chose
to stop the car and alight
for a sweet.
Hunger impelled you to those windows
behind which, around hard sandesh
and the ooze of cham cham and the yellow
puddle of rabri a haze
of insects were hovering or swimming or climbing
as on an island without a human being.
The ants, though touched
by the mishtis' resin, had
laboriously freed themselves
to ascend slopes; the flies,
enlarged by these environs, banged into each other.
I asked you how you brought yourself
to eat a specimen from that tray
—"What if there's something on it?"—
and you laughed like a girl and invoked
the Bengali imperative of hunger,
evidently more immediate than sorrow.
"I would flick it off, and eat!"
You waved away in a gesture
the invisible living creature
as if dismissing some stupid universal decorum.

Petha

You're not from these parts.

You lack the pedigree
that politesse determines.
Despite your abundance
you're made negligible
by our intolerance of translucence.

Those who love you
are a different breed.

What you are is a scandal:
the corpse of some chalkumro
turned anaemic and crystalline
as a princess's breast
and imbued with rose-water.

The middle class ignores you
and would be shocked
by how you burst in the mouth and dissolve
immediately like a thunderclap.

To My Editor

I met you over twenty-six years ago.
Your strange name preceded you.
Your fanciful grandmother
had named you "dewdrop," but
your matter-of-fact manner
was dew-like only in
its noticeable transparency
though it did hide your simplicity.
At that birthday party
of a new acquaintance's
in a first-floor room overlooking
a medieval street,
a papier-mâché butterfly
stuck vividly to a wall,
I asked to see you again.
You confess you were surprised.
Self-contradictorily,
you said later I'd always felt like family.
Your encounters with my writing
were undecided. My
nerves were jangly. At what
point you became the one
with whom I'd share my words
first, I can't remember.
The inaugural sacrifice
you made was typing out
my dissertation on a college computer.
I'm beholden to you
for deleting unneeded words
when I can't find a way of losing them.
You are merciless, sometimes

indiscriminate, about
banishing objects, even books,
you consider clutter, but
are judicious trimming content.
In spite, or maybe because,
of you astringently correcting facts, we have
been reasonably at peace for twenty-five years.

Refugees

Refugees are periodic
like daffodils.
Biennial or triennial or
recurring at great intervals
unlike daffodils
they aren't expected
or recognised when they're back.
Remember, R, two decades ago,
when we saw those nervous fairy-tale
women near Victoria,
some tired, with infants, irises
like lapis?
We'd never seen anyone like them.
We were in our thirties and easily thrilled.
They'd come out of a history book
but were ungainly and insistent
like those who find they can't find their way home.
They had enough English and gumption
to pursue you and me for money.
We dove into a black cab
and went to Highgate to have lunch with Dan.
(All of us migrants; our appointments
ascertained on the phone two weeks before.)
Months later, we saw them again
selling flowers at a traffic light.
They were still unreal, like disbanded
dancers in their headscarves
peering opportunely into car windows
or sitting, bored, with a child on the kerb.
Bosnia was on everybody's lips
and old words like Balkanisation had made a comeback.

Then, once more, they lost their modishness
and urgency.
The women must have found new clothes or
gone back home
or found somewhere to stay.

Spectacles

The twitching to existence
of a missing limb,
the abrupt reflex
of something not there
is not a memory;
it's
an expectation
of the familiar.
It—or whatever
it was that was us—
is presumably unmindful
of erasure.
A part of ourselves
at that instant registers
the absence.
Spectacles too
are a limb of sorts—
part exoskeleton,
unretractable.
When they became
my body
I neither know
nor wish to.
Momentarily seeking
my likeness in the mirror
I decide to adjust them
though they aren't there.

Creek Row

Between the road Sealdah-ward
and College Street
you are a thin, short-lived,
decaying corridor.
The point of zipping through
your oesophageal aperture
is not just to diminish
time, but tour the interior
body-part of history,
to feel no light and brush past
stone porches and unparted slats
as if one had entered
neither as spirit nor solid
the carcass of an old, old being
then burst out like a breath
into the present's pungency.

Tarting Up

It's time
to go out.
I'm not tired of writing
but
of that instant
when the book must step out again
like a woman
who rises at evening
and vacantly studies the door,
opens it, flinching
at the onrush of the street.
Before meeting the outside
you begin to tart up, choose
an eye-catching photo
for the jacket
reassessing it like a dress
you've worn many times
and finger the quotes
and snippets of praise you know
too well. They're jewels
whose beads
have minute crevasses, the thread
is loose, but you
embrace it calculatingly,
with a practised poise.
The best ones you've reserved
for tonight, when traffic
on the road's uncaring
and promising. You'll flash a smile
at him, and not look at his face.

The Left

The left
isn't the other
hand, it's the one
that's
the shadow-figure
outside the doorway—
always hovering, always near,
but instructed without edict
not to present itself.

Summoned ritually to bathe
the backside
it crouches like a Brahmin
drowning himself in dirty water
to expunge the sins of another life.

Then
after washing itself sombrely
it goes to a secluded place
where there's no danger
of being touched or noticed.

Bhim Nag

Not that deep
into the North
but it feels
the world's transformed—
the twin poles
of the handcart immovable,
pointedly thwarting
buses, robust men
unfocussed yet engrossed
in everything but the lax, neighbourly goats.
Unlike the desultory South
the road has no angles
and is interminable,
culvert-like: it and the drifting
buildings make the journey North
echo that trip to Venice—the rubbish floats
on a current.
                    Just here
processions from College Square
will veer toward the unobtrusive fork
at Nirmal Chandra Street and make their way
to Esplanade, intermittently
protesting a malignant dispensation.

Here is Bhim Nag.
Before reaching it, I tasted its doi.
A pink so shadowy it feels
the colour's all but drained away.
I pick up a pot. It's the same.
So uncannily sweet, so close to liquid,
you swallow it as it lies on your tongue.

Nothing of the outside is here.
Legends hang on walls. The interior
has, despite its abundance, the quiet
of Ramakrishna's room in Dakshineshwar.
On one half of white sandesh rose petals
rest with funereal simplicity.

Embrace This Sadness

Embrace this sadness.
You cannot embrace the sea
Or the air
But you can embrace the future
Which you turn away from
Because of its bright emptiness.
Go to it.
Embrace the sadness you feel.

Fingers

At twelve
I boycotted cutlery;
a showy rebellion against a man
who sat opposite
and didn't forgo
spoon and fork even when he was
face to face with a chicken bone.
He smiled (as he would
in tricky situations),
and raised it aloft
with prosthetic fervour.

It was then that my fingers
discovered life. They plunged into
its heat. The plate was full.
They entered the world below.
Never had they known anything
like the contact, been so close.
They eddied and circled round,
and were half drowned, half consumed,
by the element they visited.
There's no analogy
for the ensuing transformation.
Longhand writing,
for instance,
is no comparison;
longhand carried words painfully,
and didn't arrive
late, as my fingers did,
perfumed with soap, staining themselves,
stumbling, dancing in circles.

Love

So much of the world
is what we imagine.
Our illness is like love—
thirty per cent or more in the head, the rest
unresolved ailment.
And our love of this world
is an illness,
subterranean, psychosomatic, the causes
of our being here largely imaginary,
the cure often
a sudden change of location.

Chhana

It's taken me time to find
a true account
of who we are.
The provenance of the world
passed me by
till recently.
Three years ago I realised
that chhana
was not timeless.
It was
brought in by the Portuguese.
Since then I'm wondering who
the Portuguese are, and why
they are now all but forgotten.
Is chhana
a gift of consciousness;
was existence bestowed on it
by our awareness of
this curd-like mass
or was it always extraneous,
journeying
from a source?
Exactly that
question pertains
to the Portuguese—
that, not knowing them, can we
assign to them veracity?
These conundrums did not throw
me out of gear four years ago.

Can You Tell Me

Can you tell me
where to get
Mephistopheles's number?

I want to sell my soul.
It's a matter
of some urgency.

I'm not sure what it's worth,
but I've stopped
guarding it jealously.

I'm tired of walking alone.

I'm putting my soul
on the market.
Could you help me
contact Mephistopheles?

Terror (after Rustom's)

I reassess
the jar
of gajar mewa nu achar.
If I swaddle it in underwear
and secrete it in my cabin bag
will I be found out
by the hunched man at security?
Clearly, he'd be suspicious
of its chilli-sting
and the cloying sharpness of vinegar
enveloping each shaving.
I bury it till it's gone.
I weigh my chances
and look unpreoccupied.

Faltu

Why should it be
a pejorative?
Why, if I were to say
these words are *faltu*, should it
be self-deprecation?
I like the sound—so much more
personal and nearer
than "inconsequential," "waste of time,"
or "feckless."
Like a pet name
or a relative
or a small town you once visited
and remember intermittently.

Adil

He hovers over Cuffe Parade
from the eighteenth-floor balcony:
guardian, priest, and friend.
His visitors are outsiders.
His tiny wife's a "foreigner."

Once in three years I ring his bell.
When he opens the door, I lose myself
in the Sudhir Patwardhan painting.
He asks politely if I want the fan
and goes off to make Nescafé.
The ceiling is crumbling;
the floor's covered in newspapers.

What could be higher than here?
Is it any wonder when the sky falls down?
We're so far away I hear little
of the city in which I was a child.

On calm days, I see him glance
at the balcony with empathy
for sparrows that recur.
I feel a part of him
—as, in his kurta, he returns
to ask me questions—is aware
of their itinerary, and of the poems
flying in from different neighbourhoods:
they are his real guests.
Occasionally, he'll lower his mug

and sniff the air—I've never seen him smoke—
and furrow his eyebrows and smile:
"I think the city is burning."

Seeing (in) the Dark

Under the eyelid
is dark,
crouching like an insect.
Above it, making no sound,
dark rests.
The immensity
round the eye
can be gauged
by imagining darkness.
The imagination's awake:
it's aware
what's under the eyelid
inlaid with gold
is a fusion
of morning and night.
To open the eye
is as much effort
(or more)
as opening the window
to gaze from dark room
into sky,
to allow oneself to be lifted by the opposite of sight
into cool nullity.
There is no unadulterated night.
In the room
the edges of dark display
hairline cracks like an old wall.
The ceiling is absent, you only
guess, head on pillow, above
you the cushion of the universe.

Keystone

Keystone's as old as Mohenjodaro.
I summon it from a past life.
The antediluvian lampposts
dour roads and darting by-lanes
the bare ramshackle precincts in which
hydra-headed policemen
mass together to overpower
bystander and thief—
the cops' heads get lopped off
and immediately reassert themselves:
there is no time for death
where there is such confusion.
Never did crouching bystander
give the slip, never
was thief captured in Keystone—
in the scheme of things he
made his getaway. All's passed
like civilisations do: disappeared
while less tangible things persist.
There's hardly a trace of Mohenjodaro
except in books discarded or sold.

Kalbaisakhi

Inaugural uncertainty,
a shocked prelude
in which everything wavers
until the parched
prehistoric ledge
breaks out in spots: three, four,
like the leopard when it was created.
It's raining upward, drops
bruising the stone from below.
The air upon your cheek
begins to melt like ice.

The Killer Punch

The seven foot three inch
staggering grunge
punches the hero so hard
the face splashes
like it's not bone but water.
Then the perfect features
recongeal, with two strands
of hair curiously out of place.
He hits him again.
He hits *him*.
The hero's hurtling across the table
like a plate flung by a furious housewife.
He should be dead, but to our perspiring
staggering disbelief,
he rises to deliver a blow.
In life, is this possible?
Sometimes. Self-belief
and the work, if they're any good,
are weirdly absorbent.
Nothing appears
to exhaust them. They fly,
they topple, they're battered,
they get up, like it didn't matter
how often that killer punch hit home.

Ma

I said it
not really to call
or invoke:
from childhood, it's
a sigh
of wonder, an expression
of short-lived fatigue and love.
Last night I made the sound.
Shocked, I asked myself
who is listening?
Because
no one possesses
the privilege of being quite as close
and far away as she is.
Never was sign so
severed from referent,
never was word
so full of meaning again.

Sandesh

You also mean
"news."

You're news
that stays news

although chhana
goes off easily

crumbles, soon sours,
disintegrating,

regurgitated semi-solid.
Yet, first beheld,

you're an announcement.
Inhaling, we're thrown

(while it's what we expect)
by cardamom or mango

preceding you.

Tapas

Spiritual rigour
and meditation.

In Alcalá
a series
of restive visits
punctuated by introductions, laughter, and farewells.
Then an exact repetition
in a neighbouring bar.
No one stayed long.
The hellos and goodbyes
each time had the same transient forgetfulness.
No one sat.
We only stood.
The door was never too far away.
The liquor tasted of tropical
fruit, the fritters
were oddly familiar.

These were no resting places.
The point was to move on.
In Calcutta, too, sweet shops
are meant for dispersals.

And yet, in those snatched moments
of bonhomie and trade,
is there a plausible confluence
with silence and withdrawal?

Tele bhaja

The main industry
in Kolkata—
real estate
and tele bhaja.

Someone keeps launching
fritters in oil.
The tele bhaja drown,
rise steadily, and brown.

The smell of kerosene
and smoky besan
stirs this market's
appetite for itself.

Buildings arise,
flats unoccupied.
Everyone's on the pavement.
These pavements are hard to traverse.

They're where clothes are sold.
They're tunnel and arcade.
You pass one point in time
to another as you weave through stalls.

The pavement is kitchen.
The busy incursion
and extension of habitation is constant
until wherever one walks

is home.
A hand scoops potato peels
and fingers brush your breast. You notice
tele bhaja soak up the paper.

Notes in Mid-Air

In business
everyone's asleep
the bodies swaddled
but secretive
as cocoons as if they were growing
inside the blankets.
Illuminated faintly
by a sparse glow
they could be arranged
for a Beuys exhibition
or a catafalque
of luminaries.

As you waft spirit-like
through a curtain
—the barrier sufficient between two worlds—
in economy you find
the silhouettes seated, nodding
in the dark like figures in a park
after the sun's gone down.
Night has come suddenly. The aisles
are like interconnected paths
in old Europe—grandfathers
follow resolutely after infants while others sleep.
A baby's been laid flat
the way I saw
a homeless child
in Apollo Bunder
diverting herself
at midnight, outstretched
on the lamplit macadam

where her mother had placed her.
Similarly, I discover
this one before the first seat
of the first cabin
by pure accident.

The Garden Path

Making my way
from the bathroom
I realise I'm
in paradise—
not aftermath of dream,
just a flash of daylight
in which flowers in the garden path
are arranged yet not fixed
the background shot through with single birdcall
as I stumble toward bed
finding my way
from memory,
not lost or adrift, feeling an extraordinary
joy, not a euphoric pleasure, but
a balanced happiness, as if
I know, groping, I'll be here again.

Sadness-Joy

They are not different.
It's not as if
they succeed
or imitate each other.
They aren't twins
but indivisible.
Like sweet and salt, they are
one, not plural.
Impossible now
to distinguish
the lift from the fall
of gravity, the recurring pang
of loss from your healing embrace.

Ramanujan

From Nakhoda Masjid

The minarets
of Nakhoda mosque
tower over the lane—
a radio station
broadcasting from eternity.
Not far away, the Royal,
overlooking human and animal
traffic on Chitpur Road,
is still renowned for biriyani.

Maybe unduly so, since
the taste is nothing special.
On the first-floor balcony, we,
hands washed, examine
the restless concourse
like we were recent lovers
and not married for fifteen years.
The one remarkable feature,
besides the potato, are
the grains of rice, some
fat, unimpeachable white,
others a soiled modest yellow,
each unable to merge
with the other, crowded
in a neighbourly mass, yet polarised.
It's as if the atoms
married to make up space
had become visible separately,
some pure, unstained by light,
others heavy and radiant.

Ramanujan

Mahesh would cycle or simply stride
to the Broad Street Wimpy's
to get himself a beanburger.
With a wisdom not expected
of a Tamil Brahmin from Delhi
he claimed it would suffice.
In Balliol, the alternative
was jewelled Brussels sprouts and carrots
in remnants of lukewarm water.
On good days, they—the vegetarians—
might stumble upon sauerkraut
or steaming cauliflower au gratin.
You, Heeraman, chose
to forage weekly up the Cowley Road
for turmeric, rice, and chick peas
and potent jars of chana masala powder.
In the Co-op, you'd spotted "yoghurt."
It was chick peas that kept you alive.
In hall, you scrutinised the mash.
Poor Ramanujan! Seventy years
before you he must have been
the first meat-abhorring Hindu
to conjure up from odds and ends
—no spices then in Oxbridge, no
curry leaves, hardly anything
even for ordinary Englishmen
in a time of conflict and rationing—
a semblance, at odd hours of night and day,
of an aroma that half pacified
the voice that asked, *Why are you here?*

Cambridge

It took us a few days after we arrived
in the suburban flat
from which Churchill College was a glimpse away
—milk left in the fridge
by an invisible hand,
bread and jam placed recently on a kitchen shelf—
to realise Cambridge was not Oxford.
It felt more beautiful for a day.
On Madingley Road, the weather
was wet, the wind
cutting.
       Unexpectedly, the fens
became an invisible presence for us.

Then, to phrase it dramatically,
I was told I might die. I'd never felt
more well or alive (mentally,
I'd never been as out of place as in Cambridge).
From Addenbrooke's, they sent me to Papworth.

How numb we were on the eve of departure!
The journey, twenty minutes by taxi,
seemed to go on into the narrow-laned
mordant hush of a Cambridgeshire
without industry or migration: just glum stillness.
Here, past a roundabout, in a verdant
nothing, a lease of life was enforced on me.

Papworth Everard! I'd forgotten
the second, almost Gallic, half of the name.

Nothing to define it as an English village
except one Costcutter.
                    Papworth.

That was the inaugural tour. The name
would keep coming up. A few days to go,
our umbrellas drenched, heavy of foot
on Madingley Road—a taxi stopped
as if the oracle had spoken: "Do you know
the way to Papworth?" It was too much.
Defeated, we asked him to turn the car around.

Ancient wide building, the catacombs
coursing through it like veins! You and my parents
hovering at doorways, or standing, summer's ghosts,
by the curtain to my bed in the ward.
The imperial fixtures of bathtub and basin,
the unremarkable generosity of space,
and, outside, sunlight. It had stopped raining!
Despite my wakefulness that night
when I lay listening

to the woman with the smoker's rasp
remonstrating with staff recurrently,
then fell asleep, urging the dawn
to come, so I could see you
and my parents
before they took me,
despite being paraded round on a wheelchair
like a middle-aged woman in a sari
in an airport
now to X-ray, now sonography,
despite the affection I developed

for the two transplant patients who bookended my stay,
I never felt I knew the place.

I thought of Ramanujan
and the men for whom this dour house was built,
a last stop, in which the chilly breeze
through the window was therapy.
Others would sit tinkering, or daydreaming vacantly—
but Ramanujan, your spirit left your body
many times in Cambridgeshire before you went home.

Now, eighteen years after
returning one tentative afternoon
to the flat in Benians Court,
I think of Ramanujan
where I left him in Papworth,
the war ebbing, my life beginning.
I think of you too, and my parents.

That building, unsmiling memorial
to men permanently at a loose end
among whom he was strange
misfit: what will happen to it now?

Salt and Vinegar

I consumed the salt and vinegar crisps
in a single gulp.
The packet ballooned with volume
to greet me; a twin
of my stomach, but darker—
when I finished
it wasn't as empty as my stomach once had been,
my hand stretched further into it
like a glove
and came up with shards, jagged
in the depths, the world's splintered residue.

Cathedral

Not yet out of Bangalore,
muttering, "Srirangapatna!"
we glance at our watches
but want a cup of coffee.
I'm sleepy. It's quiet inside.
Old Airport Road is far away.
A man in a suit takes us in hand.
Not a cup, it's
a tumbler of brew that's spilled
into the bowl it nestles in.
Anand Bhavan.
A cathedral.
Whatever we see later—fort
or summer palace or tomb—
no mausoleum can vie
with this hive of chairs and tables.
We're doused by the coffee's perfume.
Blue and yellow letters
balloon-like float:
"High Class Veg Indian Restaurant."
Yet it's much more.
If Las Vegas were a cluster
of sweet and snack shops...Banana chips
pale as coins;
the ladies' fingers chips
teem, an infestation.
The place has the bored expectancy
dens have before play's begun.
In jukebox-like counters,
chandrakala and Bombay Halwa
and other families

of edible substances
glint like jackpot
in a slot machine.

Soon we're off to Srirangapatna again.

God

I listen for it
in my sleep-struck daze
in the toilet.
I know it'll be there
like a greeting
meant for no one else.
It's my acknowledgement
of the day
when it's taking form.
Loudspeakers demarcate the invisible
neighbourhoods, voices
orchestral, three bodiless
muezzins floating angrily
over the beaten dun-coloured
balconies
of Park Circus and Broad Street
in a web of notes.
You forget there's no other noise.

Today I heard it
in the afternoon—when,
on Sunday, these localities start
to retreat from slumber.
I like the low growl
which itself is half asleep.
Though it's in my proximity
it echoes from
the horizon of new buildings and old.

I've heard it up close
where the minaret and the middle-class lane

each pretend
the other cannot possibly exist.
In five bursts, ephemerally
but recurrently, a familiar memory:
the voice
so inhabits the ear
as an admonition
you have to shut the window; it's
full frontal din, impossible
to make sense of at close quarters.
It's as if human and God were face to face,
touching noses;
difficult to delineate features
and do much else but breathe His odour.
Yet those who live without the benefit of distance
apparently don't hear it at all.

Oxford

You know
it's two minutes away
but it takes about ten
to get in.
The train
slows down
in the night
and Oxford moves toward you
pushing
in the opposite direction; inside,
there is stoic concentration and
disbelief in these last inexplicable
moments, as if
the journey had drifted
into an iceberg
and motion
were being absorbed and buried.
Oxford looms.
It can't be seen.
With each moment
it pulverises arrival.

The Fake and the Organic

There's a kind of person
who goes to Fabindia
wearing a Fabindia kurta.
Whether the choice was predetermined
or whether, as on reaching a country
you find you're standing out
due to an unexpected familiarity,
there's an intuition, in this person
—as he weaves past the piled-up clothes—
of proprietorship and disinheritance,
of possessing what he'd come to seek,
thereby possessing nothing.
You belong here, like an edict,
flows into *You've been caught out*
as if he'd overstated
tell-tale signs of the fake and the organic.

Hamburger

Not even students dare enter
the Campus Kitchen
—once known as Zest—
after 7:45.
Nothing's left—
the salads have vanished,
various species of vegetarian puree
fill large bowls on display.
There are no diners but
a resilient Chinese youth
an Arab man
and a woman in a hijab.
No, there's a tiny English girl
flicking pictures off her smartphone.
The hamburger's been joined together
without much calculation, not with the grace
of an equation, but as if creation
were simply an act of addition.
There's a bun on top,
another below,
much like one had conceptualised a mouth
without having thought up a face.
In between, naked, no longer raw, is a tongue.
There's little to do with this mouth but
eat it—it has a taste separate
from your own cheeks and flesh. You're conscious
of not devouring yourself. You add burger sauce
from what appear like bottles of paint.
The chips you dip like swollen fingers
into the guacamole.
You're hungry—hungrier than before.

You eat with a disbelieving zest
busy in the heat of remembering.
You're immersed in a comical
misery that belongs to a very long time ago:
it must have been of importance once.
You bite; it tastes alive again.

Tunnel

The remnants of salad swim in the trough.
Entering at ten past seven,
you sense plenty's retreat.
In the furnace glow
of the hot food counter,
where, last week, you chose
a burrito lifeless
as a bandicoot, now
you point to a smudged triangle
of pizza dimpled with pepperoni.
As backup, you've banked
a bowl with couscous and a submerged layer of coleslaw.
You eat alone;
always, excess
is conjoined with impoverishment. Nothing
adds up. You pile more food.
The pizza is skin; you're sure
the fragments can be pieced together
into an anatomy
but find somehow you're at the end of it all;
the tunnel into which accumulations vanish.

Reading Kaddish

Reading *Kaddish*
after my cousin's death
I see mothers heal
even when they're fearful and mad.
Naomi is anarchic and scared
of the world—when she implodes, it's messy.
Allen is the crutch; or he thinks so.
He's full of pity and exasperation.
All the time, she remains his mother.
In this, she does what mothers do—
saves him, and envelopes him
with herself. Allen feels nothing but love.

Rereading those lines last night
for some reason on hearing my cousin died
I think of my mother in St Cyril Road
nudging me when a maidservant
who worked for her, face disfigured
by burns, would be reunited with her children.
We would ignore her, because the remnants
of the face hit us hard, but, "See,"
my mother would say, of the two
who dropped by on the way home from school,
"for them their horror-mother is everything."
For two minutes we'd be amused
by the not-so-strange, but strange, context of their
    excitement.

Kaddish, last night you taught me that
no mother can be terrible
or ugly or angry or threatening

however it seems to the onlooker.
Always, there's peace at the proximity
and certainty of the embrace.

Zombies

These four,
dumped
on the manicured shore of Eastern
Australia, are sheepish
as they struggle into uniforms
for the "cook."
Neither convict nor indentured
labour, not migrant or
native, they're ever-smiling,
sacrificial homebodies
coastline-sequestered
with access to every abundance—
shiitake mushrooms;
John Dory; anaesthetised soft-shell crab;
blow torches and blast chillers
(everything they've handled with the inborn
propriety of Picassos and children)—now
there's panic, like they're on
a liner in sight of an iceberg.
They scurry from imminent wreckage.
Tomatoes drop from hands; the cooker refuses
to catch flame—the floor shifts.
"Plate up, plate up!" The cry ripples inward.
They're coming! Suddenly you spot them.
The zombies!
Forty or fifty of them. Their serene,
irrevocable, end-of-the-world
progress ceases at the table.
Here they sit, gazing expressionlessly, as if
unaware of the passing of years. They will wait
forever, unexpectedly peaceful.

The would-be chefs are
never prepared for them, their work's
unfinished, their defences bare.
The zombies look neither deterred nor urgent.

Keith Jarrett

That grunting—
is it singing?
Or an overlay of breath
that's mostly silent
but, in the transport of playing,
becomes rasping and tuneless?
I find I'm listening less
to the magic keys
than the passionate noise of his sing-along.
I'm nervous, as I would
be about some homeless commuter
on the NYC subway
who's keeping time, shaking, oblivious
to humanity, the music all in their head.
Or does that frenzied shout
have nothing to do with anything at all—
effort; exhaustion; determination
to keep it going for another second—
like the tennis player lifting their body to serve?

Reading Li Shangyin on Emirates
While Listening to Joni Mitchell

I bypass the dragons.
The wind's tremulous.
Suddenly there's a hush
between one valley and another.
If the sun ascends a second time
after the first
will it mean day has dawned on the world?
This sound—wail of farewell
and yearning—hum of the wind—
voice in my ear—my attention lapses
momentarily—the voice says
nothing; only moans
with a reminiscent calm, cuts through the grass
from the world's edge; a thousand years later
in my immediate past
it trickles into
the ruins of poems in my hands.

Sighs, unknowing, on the alien alphabet:
("O my love, my darling,
I've hungered for your touch.")

Yesterday

Deep in the bowel of the earth
(as they say)
where it was boiling
standing once alone, once with my daughter
I noticed the Piccadilly Line's withering
over time
the way a humerus thinned
by polio
dangles in space, barely glanced at
except extensions at Heathrow
and Hounslow, phalanges
redundant but oddly firmer.

Radha, Before Term

All day she's sat in bed
laptop parted before her
like a book planted on its side
legs for hours submerged
in the quilt's blue interior—
mermaid-like
she keeps vigil
waiting maybe for no one.

At night, switching the light off
I see her face brightened
as by a hurricane lamp
eyes shining
while she looks to the horizon.

Block C

What's this building
pastel blue-white
deep modern stone
immovable,
windows throwing light sharply
during day,
reticent at night?
B's separated from C
by prehistoric water
shallow in summer
demarcated by a concrete ledge.
In it, brutalist lines
shimmer
with a vibration
that's smothered periodically
by geese;
otherwise, calm
settles on that façade
that flutters like a pennant
in a faint breeze.

Vinyl

Not the music
was the memory
but the loud scratching
at the start—
a plunge
into the realm of noise
before it becomes
melody, noise skirting silence.
The ear picked it up, and forgot
the undertone of a period—
this is what it meant
to live then on the verge, a signal
absent now—our children
needn't encounter it—
this expunging just when we begin.

The Pleistocene Epoch

To you the question came
in Norfolk or North London
gripped by the remnants
of icy sunlight—
of whether "the Pleistocene Epoch itself
has come to an end."

For me, and others
who have inherited the earth
the question is suspended. I stare out of the window
of this college room
at what can only be called
premeditated shrubbery
and note the absolute reign
of sunlight in that theatre
I once knew as a student.
A new era's at hand.

I never dreamt the day would come
when I'd ask for dark
to envelop the shrubbery:
at night, I feel its presence
but morning reassigns its place to it again.

Prynne, your life
inhabited the rim
of mine. Yet there was
obvious overlap:
we wake to the same day
yet this is where the trip
you started long ago

nears its destination;
you barely see
the sun rising on this world;
I'm stirred,
reading you,
by my immensity of loss.

The Reader

I wrote poems not for you
but presumed you'd be the reader.
Even now, these lines form
concomitant with your unknown
make-up, flesh, and DNA.
Writing is a kind of hope
as much as growing old is.
Did you grow old? Did you cross
the finishing line of youth? Are you
by chance no more? Was it
your remains I saw
the other day?
Are you, like bone, reduced
to facets of bare truth?

Onward Motion

What's this onward motion
this current—
where are we going,
me, my daughter;
tomorrow, where will she be?
I walk
up Linton Road
unobstructed
to the room
in which she's enveloped.
There's a backward motion too
imperceptible—
in the underground
when I stepped onto
the escalator
grasping the handrail
which fell behind me
while I sought it
with my hand—
steadying myself
as on a gondola
pushing forward.

Buskers

Carfax is a cross
formed by
High Street, Queen Street,
Cornmarket Street, St Aldate's.
From the apocalyptic verge
I turn
to Marks and Spencer—there
an earnest man
in black jeans
is telling a boy
without let up about Jesus.
I hear the word "Christ."
Nothing else.
Standing on one plank of the cross
at Carfax
he addresses the teenager
with soft urgency.

The buskers
on adjacent
Cornmarket Street
stand or sit a few feet apart
occupying
distinct universes.

Sometimes people encircle one and cheer.
Sometimes a girl will stop and stare.

On Cornmarket Street
they become their own tomorrow.

The audience
is an exception for those who sing.
All who play and dance
are doing it for themselves
in a haze. They cry
from a private sorrow. Listeners
loiter from morning to sundown
like walkers on a beach. A man
cradles his guitar in an alley
by the Crown, inaccessible,
like a temple carving.
     Buskers—
Tagore with his "song offerings."
Flinging them in the direction
of anyone, letting them land anywhere.

Parents

Will I see them one day
like a young soldier who's returned
home after a war
he thought would never end,
entering the hush of the drawing room
to find them sitting there?

Chalta

Woman's an animal with language.
When she pushes the *chaltar ambal*
toward me
I view the green soup
with scepticism.
She confesses: "I have it to chew
the *chalta*"—
whereas, I
reserve my mouth to swallow words
hardly ever putting my teeth to use.
She, though, can issue
such articulations and immediately
forget them as she destroys
the rind to make
the juice she ruminates over on her tongue.

Tuchchho Kobita

I like the word "tuchchho."
It contains its pride.
Its insubstantiality
opposes its true being.
What it states
is what it tastes
of: a fleeting sweetness.
How can what's
tuchchho be homeless?
It's always close, like an only
child. We never beget epics.

Daybreak 1st January

From light's margin
comes your coughing.
I grasp sleep. Awash, I cherish
and resist your closeness. You
shudder gently, supine.
I hear the repeated pairs—
cough, cough; cough, cough;
the glue of sleep competes
with the longevity
of sound, breath, all we know—
cough, cough. You are life—
life, loyally, has woken us,
though, curled up, we pretend
we're root; as unrelated
as bodies are, parallel
and horizontal, are the disruptions
of declamations; bird-cry.
I embrace them, since they're mine
as much as your cough is mine
to receive and yours to release
then let them go and surrender
this spasm of breath and love
to what of course we have no memory of.

Eating at Home

The more my daughter eats out
the more it feels food at home
has got better. When did we last taste
this extraordinariness at a stretch?
My mother's no longer alive.
Even when she was, I can't remember
such an uninterrupted and unthreatened
phase, when the seasoning
and spices were
unimprovable, the out-of-season jackfruit
and chhana full of auburn colour a return
to existence; the bhetki fried
in parcels of pumpkin leaves
has a freshness that can't derive from ingredients alone.

For visitors my wife brought out
a pot of tamarind chutney
made when my mother was there.
The coarse gur-coated chhara was hair
unspooling from an atavistic scalp
that in time grew
sweet-sour: we eat our forebears.
I'm sure about nothing. I can't say
how long it will last, or if we're
in an era with no justification.
Something is being given
to us in a middle period in which
our lives are changed but we are not,
my parents have receded, we are guests at home,
our bodies work (we possess them fully);
our daughter, grown, is semi-absent—

I wonder if she'll stay unmindful of this food
in her experience of winter—will
the cook leave us one day, as my parents did?

Mother

"Mother" was simply one of you—
with that funny nose
the freckled tip,
your exacting littleness.
The manifold stick-on teep on the forehead.
You were a singer.
From diaphragm up and down
you were music: clear, surprising tone.
I feel now I'd encountered you
at other times—"force of nature" is said
glibly of many, and was only part-true of you.
I would have recognised you in forms
immaterial, material, human and
old and insentient; prescient, I saw
you before knowing it was you,
and, retrospective, in the aftermath,
found you again, even when I didn't
know you, I knew you were before me;
"mother" was only one of you—
that printed silk sari, the low-heeled sandals—
you were multiple, too diverse,
for me not to have, in this world and others,
forgotten you, fallen into your presence.

Post-Midnight, Rain

It's not "sound"
but low-pitched white noise.
Onset of silence
that wasn't there
a second ago
underneath
the swing
and abrupt intake of breath
of air-conditioning,
the memory
of machinery—
the overhead fan,
quiet as a bird
flying in the dark—
behind these, an absence,
absolute and brief.

Apartment

Like a labourer
stooping
in the odour
of work
or a fishmonger's pores
admitting without hindrance
the smell of scales
every being
in the apartment
lives blind
on the oxygen
of chicken curry
for days.
It's irrevocably
in the towel—
burnt cinnamon sticks,
turmeric,
garlic, and onions—as in a shallow
of breath, the soft
perspiring cloth
pressing damply on the face.

Sandesh Mould

Furtive as a sea horse
or something
that's danced underwater
to a current
outside time and light
to survive
as residue—
one a brooch, another
as corpse
of fish or mango,
yet another
with the submerged finality
of a seal,
each form
shakes itself free
to swim away—are you
then cradle or
exoskeleton:
are you finished, or about to begin?

Orange Juice Concentrate

Orange juice concentrate
I had
in 1973
in a crystalline land.
I know now
it wasn't juice at all
but pale gasoline
to scour throats
and oesophagi
of an unprecedented machinery.
You didn't think of oranges
when drinking it; in fact,
you didn't drink it any more
than a machine swigging
down oil drinks fire; tasting nothing
but the habit of replenishment.

They

They would come
from Chandannagar
the thumb-sized
patal, man's creation, not
nature's, the
stony custard apples.
Near them
the karhais,
spatulas,
child-size, possessed
by an over-reigning normalcy.
Satisfying no hunger
but of seeing—
the dissociated gaze's
appetite for existence.

To a Poem

Where were you?
Three weeks went
and I missed you not knowing it.
Always the fear,
the speculation,
illogical, plausible,
of not finding you again.
Even now, I'm not sure
it's you who are returning
to my life. But anticipation's
already made you possible, and
possibility brings joy.

Death-Song

Having been called
to sing
at an auditorium
where music
will indent
the obituary, I speculate
whom I will sing to.
Is it you, absent one
whom I knew in person hardly—
your smile floats
away; it's the only
thing that escapes you—or
is it the living
who gather to take in the song?
Not quite music, it's something else
wrenched from situation and whatever life-
experience gave birth to melody.
It's not intended to survive.
It dies to engender.

Dhak

On the eighth day at six o'clock. On the ninth day at seven.
Roughly thirty seconds. Approaching with what must only
be merriment. I don't open my eyes; I smile in half sleep.
The tattoo not just sacred, but comic. *They're so funny, all
of them*, I think, of the living dhaki and his assistant and the
fictional entourage. Takta-tatak—takta-tatak: impossible to
take seriously. It's intrusive, sweetly mocking, like a finger.
A mother's smile when you fall. You get up, teeter forward.
Takta-tatak, it says; and is gone. You hear it the rest of the
day, like your cell phone when it's on silent. You don't find
it in temple or court. It's the fag-end of a fairy tale.

Life-line

for my father-in-law

Randomly promoted
to business class
I lie recumbent
on being airborne.
My feet go into a cavern.
I lose my shoes.
Prostrate, I weigh memories:
they come, unheralded,
between images on the screen.
At this altitude, they have
no history.
I can't judge
which is older—walking
down Park Street, or waking
next to you early this morning.
I'm ill.
Sunk in comfort, I stare
at the filaments
of my life-lines:
the charger's cord; the remote control's
shoelace-thick wire;
the unentangled reel
to my headphones.
They drip, drip, drip
life into my horizontal body
or do I eke into
them the resistance I'd hoarded?
A small light I haven't seen before
is keeping vigil above.

Our Parents

How embarrassing they are!
Some of their views
can be extraordinary.
Increasingly, we were torn
between protecting and
disowning them
for at least fifteen minutes.
In the end, when they left,
it had little to do with us.
They don't stick to a plan.
On one level, so focussed
on organising our lives,
on another, as it turns out,
unreliable in their departure.

Short Q and A

Q. How do you know if you're an experimental filmmaker?

A. If, after decades of making cinema and receiving acclaim and honours, the Damocles of uncertainty hangs on you as you begin your new film just as it did when you'd made your first, if there is no guarantee that it will be shown in cinemas or even seen, you can conclude with some certainty that you're an experimental filmmaker.

Q. Who or what is a poet?

A. A poet is a religious figure. That is to say, the voice of the poet can't be heard. This leads to the purity of the line.

Q. Who or what are men?

A. Men are those who create and break the laws.

Q. Who or what is a human?

A. A human is one who can bear infinite pain.

Q. What is an endorsement?

A. An endorsement is the death of championing.

Q. What do the words "the people" mean?

A. They are a justification for any and every action. But Mandelstam uses them without justification when he claims "The people need poetry that will be their own secret / to keep them awake forever."

Q. What excites a writer most?

A. Making another poem.

Q. What's to be made of J, the Indian critic who has no compunction about writing forewords and essays on any writer, artist, or filmmaker, notwithstanding what he feels about them, for money?

A. Well, he insists on getting paid. There's no shortage of people who do the same for nothing.

Q. In what way are you different from Mr Bean?

A. He detests Charlie Chaplin.

Q. What causes most distress in a writer's legacy?

A. Their "politics." Far from causing revulsion, bad
   writing is hardly noticed.

Q. What might be an instance of a backhanded compliment?

A. "I admire your optimism."

Q. What's the difference between a writer's work and their reputation?

A. A writer's work provokes envy or calculated indifference; elicits admiration or a desire to emulate. A writer's reputation is wedded to legitimacy. It's why we ask for endorsements from writers we may have never read and may never read.

Q. Who or what is a racist?

A. Someone who believes in human values for people with their own set of features. A woman standing in a queue, making baby-sounds to an infant, glowered when she saw me. Selective humanity undermines more than terror.

Q. How might a "person of colour" temporarily hold off a violent white racist?

A. By laughing at his racist jokes.

Q. Why would a "person of colour" laugh at racist jokes?

A. To stave off an attack and (as no one can fake such responses) because he found them funny.

Q. Why would he find them funny?

A. Because every intelligent person feels moments of disgust towards his own community, and a joke relieves that anger.

Q. When would someone say, "Take out your penis"?

A. In a rushed preamble to lovemaking.

Q. When else?

A. In a different kind of emergency, to check if you're Muslim or Jewish.

Q. Which answer is okay for the first but not for the second?

A. "I'll show you mine if you show me yours."

Q. Why is "Hit the Road Jack" so short?

A. Because life makes no sense.

Q. What is an instance of a fundamental desire that is realisable and has been set aside through forgetfulness?

A. When I was a boy, I dreamed of having a beard. I thought today, "I've always been clean-shaven."

Q. What's your top priority when you're in the West?

A. To finish the dishes.

Q. What do managers manage?

A. The imagination. Before them, it ran wild.

Q. Why does the writing feel tired when you write for too long?

A. Because the imagination is a muscle.

Q. What is required to maintain an acceptable standard of morality?

A. A scapegoat.

Q. Who is impossible to sentimentalise?

A. Your mother, as she's the first being in whom you learn to love imperfection.

Q. What is "savouring"?

A. A return to life. You're reunited with the quotidian. You savour its taste, which you'd forgotten, without constraint.

Q. Why is there a shortage of mental health institutions to "normalise" aberrant behaviour?

A. The task of "normalisation" has passed to universities and corporations.

Q. What's the difference between playing a part on the stage and playing one in "real life"?

A. The actor is unmindful of their audience.

Q. Can you have a true sense of sorrow if you live in extraordinary privilege?

A. Think of Gautama.

Q. What is an archive?

A. The past.

Q. What is poetry?

A. A form of subtraction where words are viewed as impediments.

Q. Who might we say led a life of privilege?

A. Walter Benjamin.

Q. What is privilege?

A. Privilege is what fails to protect us.

Q. What is the worst thing about American winters?

A. Wearing thermals in a heated room.

Q. What's the difference between epic theatre and realist theatre?

A. Epic theatre gives to us for the hundredth time a story we know. We have even memorised its lines. Realist theatre gives us a "new" story that confirms the conventions we're schooled in. We go to epic theatre for the already known. We go to realist theatre for the expected.

Q. Which question have you been asking yourself lately?

A. "I wonder if I'll miss Amy Robbins?"

Q. Who is Amy Robbins?

A. Someone who disapproves of me intellectually, and whom I hope never to run into after two months.

Q. Why are you wondering if you'll miss her?

A. Because, although it's hard to love everyone, it's possible to miss anyone or anything.

Q. Define a particular spiritual need.

A. The desire to not understand at once.

Q. Was this what Pound meant when he wished for *The Waste Land* a not "single and unique success"?

A. Hard to be sure.

Q. When Eliot called Pound *"il miglior fabbro,"* did he mean Pound had imparted some clarity to his poem?

A. Unlikely.

Q. Why is craft spiritual?

A. Because it devises ways to conceal meaning.

Q. Does concealing meaning require craft?

A. Yes. It's near-impossible to speak without meaning
something.

Q. Name a difference between summer and winter.

A. Smells move faster in summer, sounds in the winter.

Q. What's another name for the future?

A. The past. It's where you encounter yourself.

Q. The future has already happened?

A. No. But you'll recognise neighbourhoods you're still to visit.

Q. What is value?

A. Value is a kind of understanding that comes when ties are loosened. It's a piece of music whose beauty you for some reason ignored most of your life.

Q. What is research?

A. Research is what you've learnt from past lives. Your memory of it is vague, but it gives you an affinity for certain lived concepts.

Q. Who are a saint's first followers?

A. His teachers. They are his first audience.

Q. Who asks the questions?

A. This is information I can't share with you.

St Cyril Road

and Other Poems

The Village

And my father was a student back in the fifties,
in London (picture in overcoat and tie
and casual umbrella), migrating (like a bird
without the essential discipline of a bird)
from digs to digs, bedsitter to bedsitter,
yet unmarried to Mother, absent and lonely
as Adam in a foggy paradise when Eve
was uncreated, until mother arrived
and something grew complete. Both went for clear
monastic walks down grey, washed London lanes.
And once they took a friend's mother—a Swiss
lady—wizened, but not, I imagine, in her dotage—
who, while they walked in the distance, attently painted
Hampstead Heath. The world was all before them.
Finished on an eventless day in the fifties, she
gifted it to them. They brought it back to India.
It hangs upon the wall inside my room...
It's painted on an ochre background. Two white, two grey
afterthoughts are clouds or a mass of clouds.
Below this, there's the Heath, but to those people
who haven't seen the Heath (as once I hadn't),
it looks like a village, the kind of village Rip
van Winkle must have returned to when he woke.
A village, then. A house and a lost church
defined by a tapering spire, are visible. Trees
are smudges, like green, dark green thumbprints on paper.
In fact, the village is a smudge held in the stillness
and clarity of her thought. This could be a day
near autumn, when the leaves haven't fallen, but are
    about to,
or a day in summer, spent thinking of rain, and rain

about to fall. Or a brightish day in winter.
It's not spring; spring's about to come, or gone.
I can picture that world and the warm, freckled hands
that gave it colour, or restraint from colour, which is the
    deepest
colour of all. As a boy, that scene, enframed,
was, for me, England. In a way, it still is.
Growing up and taking the trouble to see the real thing
hasn't diminished the village, its heart as full
of sleeping resonance as the unstruck church bell.

1986

St Cyril Road, Bombay

Every city has its minority, with its ironical, tiny village
fortressed against the barbarians, the giant ransacks and
    the pillage
of the larger faith. In England, for instance, the "Asians"
    cling to their ways
as they never do it in their own land. On the other hand,
    the Englishman strays
from his time-worn English beliefs. Go to an "Asian"
    street
in London and you will find a ritual of life that refuses to
    compete
with the unschooled world outside. In Bombay, it's the
    Christian minority that clings
like ivy to its own branches of faith. The Christian boy
    with the guitar sings
more sincerely than the Hindu boy. And in St Cyril Road,
    you're familiar
with cottages hung with flora, and fainting, drooping
    bougainvillea,
where the noon is a charged battery, and evening's a
    visionary gloom
in which insects make secret noises, and men inside their
    single rooms
sing quaint Portuguese love songs—here, you forget, at
    last, to remember
that the rest of Bombay has drifted away, truant, and
    dismembered
from the old Bombay. There, rootless, garish, and widely
    cosmopolitan,
where every executive is an executive, and every other
    man a Caliban

in two-toned shoes, and each building is a brooding tyrant
    that towers
over streets ogling with fat lights… Give me the bougain-
    villea flowers
and a room where I can hear birds arguing. I won't live in a
    pillar of stone,
as ants and spiders live in the cracks of walls, searching
    for food alone
in the sun-forgotten darkness. That's why I've come to St
    Cyril Road
to lose myself among the Christians, and feel Bombay like
    a huge load
off my long-suffering chest. Woken up at six o'clock in the
    morning,
by half-wit birds who are excited in the knowledge that
    day is dawning
on the sleeping lane—that's what I want. The new day
    enters my head
like a new fragrance. I rise, dignified, like Lazarus from the
    dead.

1985

The Bandra Medical Store

When I first moved here, I had no idea whatsoever
where the Bandra Medical Store really was. But someone

in the house was ill. So I ventured out, let my legs
meander to a chosen path, articulate their own distances.

I guess my going out for the medicine, even the illness,
    were just
excuses for me to make that uninsisting journey

to a place I hadn't seen. Two roads followed each other
like long absences. The air smelled of something not
    there. Branches

purled and knitted shadows. There was a field, with a
    little landslide
of rubble, and a little craggy outline of stone.

I drifted past heliotropic rubbish-heaps, elderly
white houses. An aircraft hummed overhead. And did

the houses look like rows of slender barley from the pilot's
window, row pursuing row, held in a milieu of

whiteness, unswayed by a clean, flowing wind?
Then the plane donned a thick cloud. All it left was a
    cargo

of loaded silence. I supposed that I must be lost.
It grew evening. Trees fluttered in the dusk-sough

like winged, palaeolithic moths eddying towards
the closing eye of the sun. I asked someone, "Do you know

where the Bandra Medical Store is?" The directions
he gave me were motionless gestures scrawled on

a darkening fresco. I stepped forward, intentionally
trampled a crisp leaf, which then made the only

intelligible comment of the evening. But I took care
not to squash a warrior-ant that scuttled before me.

He was so dignified, so black. Had I been smaller, I'd have
ridden him back home, or off into the sunset.

1986

St Cyril Road Sequence

I. MIDDAY

The incantatory beating of a hammer
against a rock, and two birds cleave the field of air.
The sun sits in the garden, while the gardener
cuts and piles up grass, and leaves the flowers
secure, untouched. A woman sweeps the courtyard,
unsettling bedded, impermanent blankets of dust
and silence. And I'm lulled by the sound of workmen
delving the road. Their cloudy, metal clanging
apotheosises rest, like a recurrent Chinese
gong. I can't see them—I think of their silhouettes
flashing in the heat, bodies bent like ciphers.
Each sound lacks permanence, each wakeful image,
in its sharp flowering and fading to a zero
in this white, sun-white noon, is a constant loss
of itself, and then a recovery, a glowing echo
surfacing from a dark, centreless well.
Twice, with my sense-heavy eyes, I notice,
along a muffled world of toylike objects,
the tangent outline of a dragonfly
against a leaf, its wings whirring so fast
you can hardly see them unless you imagine
their balance between urgency and composure.
Catch one, and knot a thread around its end,
and you can fly it like a kite. Let it go,
and it'll glide off, diminishing with mournful elegance,
the thread lagging behind it like a vapour-
trail spuming from a low jet ribboning the sky.

Meanwhile, I fall asleep. Like a film of dust
that's absorbed the seven colours, quietly, the dragonfly,
the cut grass, the echoing workmen, and a reticence,
settle imperceptibly on my black pupils; these
are twice born in my sleep; when I wake
the lonely road crumbles before my eyes.

2. EVENING

But beyond this lintel-slender lane,
surprising as a sliver of sunlight between curtains, faint
as a yellow route of light no one dare tread on,
            are the larger roads that course
like dark honey out of a honeycomb towards traffic lights,
                        wheeling intersections,
and all is a carnival.
                    At sunset, they say it's, do you
know, they say it's the "peak hour," and the cars
swim like red or silver fish past the junctions,
and the lights shudder on in shops, re-creating golden
    afternoon.
But in this lane, the light of the sun goes out, and
little islands of fluorescence shine in the rooms behind
    windows,
and pigeons stop quarrelling and mating, or mating and
    quarrelling,
and a mathematical progression of birds and insects
dissolve into their imprecise, unlit shadows.
What elsewhere, everywhere, in the hot crucible of the
    city, is the "peak hour,"
is here the casual, trickling moment of
gradual anticlimax,
the levelling

of shadows into shadow, the moment
when the old Parsi lady interrupts
the impractical river of talk
from her unmarried brother-in-law, and says:
"You must stay for dinner. You mustn't leave without
    dinner... "
and there is a pause in the conversation of the world.

3. SUNDAY

Morning, and the mist ripples back to the unexpected
    roofs like a flock of endless, white
gulls, circling to rest. And a galaxy of dew and insect
    glistens, as trees arrive silently
out of the moist darkness, and this slow-flowering steam
    wavers from my coffee cup. Then
the single bread of peace is broken and disturbed this
    Sunday, peace broken into
pieces, and the fine, too-delicate crumbs rain on the earth
    where the earth opens like
a grateful palm. Never to have lived is best. And the
    second best
        is to grow old with the morning into
afternoon, and then to evening, when sundry shadows and
    gestures marry
        like the vanished divisions of a shut fan.
        This Sunday raptness, this biblical
quietude unlabouring in waves, the crows prearranged on
    the boughs, the leaves
        a parrot-green, and the flies relearning
a disciplined dance... No movement but this dance, no
    movement
        but a mimicry of shadows. And no voice

to be heard but the newspaper's, as it crackles peremptorily in
an old man's tangled fingers.

4. COMMUNITY

In the oldest, bunched houses with tottering stairs,
the Christians live, like prophets dedicated
to the cause of being obscure. The men with guitars,
the old women knitting... all their lives, they've waited.

Here, lining the lane at systematic intervals,
the bruised bungalow squat with a wild beard of grass
in the gardens, and watered-down, twenty-watt bulbs
shine in the verandas. Around them, a mass

of tall coloured buildings rise, as each timid bungalow
is emptied, and Christians who lived behind those doors
generations together, now old as weed, sell their land
and property for drink. Their houses come down on all fours.

In their place, the large buildings burgeon with neat
rectangular gardens. I myself live in one.
But occasionally, I scan the lettering on those gates
—Helen Villa, Rose Cottage—ironically dark in the sun.

5. AFTER MIDNIGHT

Last night, the medallion moon was caught oddly
between sleek, glowing channels of telegraph wire.
No one stirred, but a pacific of lights went on burning
in the vacant porches, the garages. I imagined
an impassioned movement beneath the still surface,

as if ants were travelling by hidden routes under
the sleeping earth, or a fin was dipping again, again,
past the calm skin of water. Twice, I sensed hands,
behind windows, strike a match, and a swift badge of flame
open and shut like a hot mouth. Later, ghosts
of dead Christians, dead animals, returned to displace
a leaf, to push a gate, and to knock on the silence
of the living. A worried wind scuttled past the schoolyard,
shadows slept on gaping church benches. Meanwhile,
the stars blinked, small, valedictory beads of moisture
on a surface of melting glass. Then the watchman
sojourned through the lane, tapping the walls and the
    lampposts
with a stick straight and mutely resonant, startling,
no doubt, frogs and bandicoots in their homely undergrowth
by the gutter. Around him, the heavy trees bent their
    necks—
swans at the edge of a dark lake. I stood and listened
to the slow and solitary rhythm of his stick, as it spoke
and spoke again, then again, each brief pellet of sound,
insufficient, but accurate as a metronome keeping
time, while a reluctant child practices scales.
Eloquently, it faded, dim, repetitive, metallic,
tick... tick... rick... tick... in the purblind darkness,
then nothing. Only the faint, circular ticking of my
    wristwatch,
where the white, radium-pointed arms on the grey dial
changed from minute to minute, conceiving morning.

1986

Letter from the Hills

So yesterday, at last, we made a clean breakaway.
There are times one *has* to leave Bombay behind.
And so we drove up the Western Ghats to Lonavala
through a road hewn rudely and gutted from rock.
Reaching there or leaving home early in the morning
wasn't as important as the sense of travelling like a breath,
pure and substanceless, further and further from the body
that gasped it angrily. There were others like us
in their cars, headlights streaming in the morning-mist's
    dragnet.
(I once saw, on film, reindeer migrating past
a cold tract of land. Their swarming eyes kindled
into torches. Their bodies formed a galloping mist
that shrouded the earth.) As the sun came up, we
saw the leaves peer out, shivering. Each leaf nurtured a
    dewdrop
and a sly caterpillar. The fields strode into view
with peasants on their backs, and a mute school of taxis
flickered by us, intent as black-and-yellow beetles.
Twice, in those fields, we saw how the poor live
tranquil as ghosts behind a magic chalk circle
they never transgress. But later, near the fisheries
the poor became a way of life, like the smell
of fish drying, and raw grass. We crossed the long bridge
above the Thane Creek, where the leviathan Arabian Sea
narrows itself to a whisper. At the end, rafts lay, delicate
as flecks of dried paint on a wet, just-begun painting.
A fly travelled with us. Four times, it tried to leave
but crashed into the glass. Then it explored the window
as if it were a lucent membrane, and combed it questioningly.
After a while, it rested, gripping its escarpment

like a pebble in a waterfall, or a speck of dust hanging
in a vertical wall of light. Outside, the morning landscape
changed its bright currency. Then, we climbed up the
    mountains
and a gorge unseamed *below*. And our car was like the fly
stuck to its patch of nothingness, and white clouds were
    horses
that neither whinnied nor stamped, but only breathed halos
of steam and cold vapour. If I could capture that instant
like a lone, tremulous dewdrop pinned to the green
scroll of a leaf, I would send it back to you
sealed in this envelope. Instead, I send you this poem.

1986

o

Afternoon Raag

in memory of Pandit Govind Prasad Jaipurwale
(1944–1988)

The doorbell rings. The music teacher comes in.
He is smiling as usual. His body is smiling. He is hum-
    ming a complicated tune—
Outside, wind, light, and rain revolve the landscape in a
    shifting treadmill of shadow.
Inside, in the cool room, my mother and the music teacher
    sit on the carpet, as usual,
enclosed, in the drawing room, by sofas and tables and
    paintings and curios.

My mother plays the harmonium; she begins to sing.
Her fingers on the black-and-white keys make, of her
    hand, a temple with many doors.
When the music teacher joins in intermittently, he shows
    what a strange thing the human voice is,
this tiny instrument in the throat, with its hidden universe
    of notes, its delicate, inscrutable laws.
A raag, spacious as the mansion the rain builds, unfolds—
    and sighs, like one of the elements.
Inside the great architecture of the raag, through the clear
    archway of notes, world without humans,
two figures sit, each alone
—my mother and the music teacher—enclosed by sofas
    and paintings and curios.

The music teacher is listless today.
He does not respond.
My mother is just a little irritated as she sings, but she is
    afraid, too, of something she does not understand.
The music teacher has merged with the sofa behind him,

momentarily indistinguishable from the soft, indifferent contours of the furniture,
with the disturbing patience and resignation of furniture.
His wife, his widowed mother, his brother, his brother-in-law, his sister, his four children,
the jewelled constellation that appeared at his birth,
are moving away from him. He is alone, sitting on the carpet, leaning his back against the sofa.
Behind this moment of serenity in this small, calm room,
with its clear, cool space flowing in and out of a listlessness,
is something liquid and grieving, something that cannot tolerate its own shimmering presence,
but melts away from itself all the time, like the giant walls of rain, or tears, or something else.

The music teacher is dying.
He does not know it, but he will be dead in less than a year's time.
He will not see the rain again.
He does not know it. His ignorance of death surrounds him like a halo, an intimacy with God.
My mother does not know it.
The rain does not know it.
The world is being washed clean by the rain. Something in us, human but one with the season,
is also being washed clean, tear after tear, cloudburst in silence.

Nothing remains but the human voice, this tiny instrument inside the throat
endeavouring to carry a world inside it. Then, that too becomes silent.
The raag, self-created galaxy of notes, sigh of the elements, sighs like the rain, passes into nature.

We do not see him. My mother goes on singing, as if
    unaware. He moves further away, not drawing attention
    to himself.
We do not see him now, except as a shadow against the sofa,
merged with the furniture, the endless meditation of
    furniture,
his lungs filled with water, his face and feet swollen and
    his mouth smiling,
become one with the reverie of furniture.
My mother sits there, singing, the rain falls, melting from
    its own presence,
the moment perfected not by art but by mortality, the
    mortal moment, repeating and repeating its own life.

1989

Kitchen

These memories are melodies
you sing to yourself when you choose.
Dishes and pots left to dry,
moisture, and the gleaming hands
working like music, a servant's
slow voice in a child's ear
as water overflows mournfully.
And the old homelovingness
of light falling and touching the black
utensils; the bee-buzz of love,
part song, part nature's reverie.

1990

September

A ladder set against a grey sky.
The road small and quiet; the smell of hot tea.
Will it rain today?—possibly.
The wind's warm, as wet as July.

It's only eleven a.m. The man
on the ladder tries to fix a light on the post.
His pyjamas flicker; innocent ghost!
floating twenty feet above where the ladder began.

The washerman and the watchman sip their tea.
They exchange a joke. The washerman smiles.
When the light burns, this morning, you see it for miles.
The ladder rests, darkly and angularly.

1990

Nissim Ezekiel

This man, in a room full of papers
in the Theosophy Building,
still young at fifty-five
the centre of his small universe
told me, for fifteen minutes,
that my poems were "derived."
I was seventeen.
I listened only to the precision
of his Bombay accent, juxtaposed
in my mind with the syllables of his name.
In some ways, he did not disappoint.
I went out and had a cup of coffee
at an Udipi restaurant
and did not see him again
until seventeen years later in Paris
when he recognized my name
but had forgotten who I was.

2000

Morola Fry

These small freshwater fish
that are eaten whole—head, tail,
backbone, not to speak of the flesh,
are fried in hot oil,
four or five held together
in a binding of chopped onions and flour
which apparently sews them together into islands
from which their crowded eyes stare like jewels.

2000

How Do You Fight This Monster?

How do you fight this monster?
Three years into the new century,
you pick up a handful of stones from the street.
You secrete boxcutters and wires.
A penknife lies warm in your hand.

You wake up in the morning, eat breakfast,
go out of the house and explode.

The generals have an inexhaustible arsenal
of names: "imperialist villains...
criminals...cowards...idiots..."

Sticks, stones, and names.

2003

Uncollected Poems

The Writers

On constantly mishearing "rioting"
as "writing" on the BBC

There has been writing for ten days now
unabated. People are anxious, fed up.
There is writing in Paris, in disaffected suburbs,
but also in small towns, and old ones like Lyon.
The writers have been burning cars; they've thrown
homemade Molotov cocktails at policemen.
Contrary to initial reports, the writers
belong to several communities: Algerian
and Caribbean, certainly, but also Romanian,
Polish, and even French. Some are incredibly
young: the youngest is thirteen.
They stand edgily on street-corners, hardly
looking at each other. Long-standing neglect
and an absence of both authority and employment
have led to what are now ten nights of writing.

2005

Balthazar

In another birth
I was
Balthazar.
In this birth,
I still have
his arbitrary appetites,
his self-absorption,
his unquestioning
trust in human beings.

2021

Recovery

After spells
of obsessive work

God starts feeling out of sorts
and

falls back.
The eyelids
aren't
enough to shut out light.

Eyes closed, drifting in
a red haze, he listens
to pigeons. For a while, stays
awake, free of the world.

2021

Amazing Sleeplessness

In darkness I lie.
It's not that
my mind's
still working.
No, it's
soaring with thoughts,
gone off like
Superman
diving up
to the remotest bit of sky.
Lonelier than motorway
or by-lane are the spaces
Superman roams,
eyes cast
on the planet
in its entirety.
From that height, he gazes
not only on geographies
but histories that have come and gone,
then plummets
to my window—
he has suddenly
thought of me
alone below: he hovers
wide-eyed, shy;
with his cape
envelopes my gratitude.
I've rushed to him—"Lois,"
he murmurs—I can't
subsist without him, then

he lifts me, springs
miles up,
restive until
he's shown me
all of the universe.
I'm secure
in his arms
for the time
we hang in nothingness.
My body lies outstretched
—a drunk on a pavement—
about to pass out but transfixed
by Superman and me. Neither
he nor I notice it.
The more we range
above the world
with untrammelled ease
the more exhausted it becomes.

2021

Forgotten Poems

It surfaces,
a line, or a poem—
decades old.

From within the anthology
the poem springs up.
It opens, again,
a path.
      "Jata mat
tata path"—because the poems
are quests,
varied, crowded,
each is valid
as any religion.

Jata mat
tata path: who remembers
these teeming short-lived faiths?—

I hold it
in my palm—it takes
me minutes to finish:
one of thousands
of forgotten poems,
like any faith
each indisputable.

2022

Chhena Sandesh Bhubaneshwar

Little of the inexhaustible
grime in the world
can stain
its firm, yielding grain.
It's as if the caviar of
its surface became a filtering
machine, kidneys
flushing out darkness.
In each minute component
it stays, contra the world,
chronic, resolute white.

2022

Cold Soup

"Imaginary gardens
with real toads"—does
that include the taste
of soup which in
the story
has just been served, but by
the tenth take's gone creamy and cold?
Dinnertime is garden
in which the character sits; the toad's
invisible, private to
the actor's stoic moment
of tasting;
I wonder if this,
too, is poetry.

2023

Clothes-drying

Where do I put them?
Everywhere.
But first I retrieve
the racks—
part rib cage, part
derelict Christmas trees
and hang on them
as if it were
the festive season underwear,
vest, hanky, kurta—
the maisonette, upper
and lower floors, is populated
with celebratory ornaments
thrown on all
surfaces;
even the bannister's wrapped
in pillow cases and duvet covers—
only the pyjamas
are martyrs; they're crucified on
heaters no longer in use this summer;
they're defeated, pure; they've given up
their soul to a truth that we
no longer can give credence to.

2023

Translations from Bengali

Seven Songs by Rabindranath Tagore

1

Such compassion, o compassionate one!
Touched by pure rays, my heart—like a lotus—
    blossomed at your feet.
Within, without, I've glimpsed you—in this world,
    and other worlds, and the ones to come—
in shadow, light, happiness, grief, seen you,
in tenderness, love,
suffusing the universe and my wakefulness.

1897

2

I could speak to her on a day like this,
on a day when it rains as heavily.
You can open your heart on a day like this—
when you hear the clouds as the rain pours down
in gloom unbroken by light.

Those words won't be heard by anyone else;
there's not a soul around.
Just us, face to face, in each other's sorrow
sorrowing, as water streams without interruption;
it's as if there's no one else in the world.

This earthly web's as untrue
as the constant noise of life.
Only our eyes drinking their own nectar

as the heart feels what's only true to the heart—
all else melts in the dark.

Surely no one in this world would come to harm
if I rid my mind of this burden?
If I said a couple of words to her
in one corner of this room in Sravan's downpour
surely the world would remain unaffected?

The day passes in anxious waves
lit by flashes of lightning.
Now's the time it seems I could say
the words that, all my life, I'd kept to myself—
on such a day, when it rains heavily.

1889

3

The sky full of the sun and stars, the world full of life,
in the middle of this, I find myself—
so in wonder my song awakens.

The blood in my veins reproduces the measure
of waves of infinite time to whose ebb and flow earth sways—
so in wonder my song awakens.

I've pressed on each blade of grass on the way to the forest,
my heart's lifted in madness, dazzled by the scent of flowers,
all around me lies this gift, outspread—
so in wonder my song awakens.

I've listened closely, opened my eyes; poured life into the
    earth,
in the midst of the known looked for the unknown,
so in wonder my song awakens.

1924

4

You may as well sit beside me a little longer,
        if you have something to say, say it now.
See—Sarat's sky begins to pale,
        the vaporous weather makes the horizon shine.
I know you'd longed to see something,
that's why you came to my door at dawn,
did you see it before daylight faded again?
        Tell me, traveller—
for that thing, at the most unapproachable reaches
of myself, has blossomed like a flower in my blood.

Full of doubt, you've still not entered my room,
        you made music lightly in the courtyard outside.
What will you take with you when you go abroad?
        Dear guest, this is the last hour of farewell.
In that first hour of dawn, when you put your work to one
    side
and set out in search of that profound
message, did you find any hint of it anywhere?
        Tell me traveller—
that message, lighting its hidden fire
in my blood, burns its lamp with the flame of my life.

1928

5

What you wrote has, in the dust, turned to dust.
The letters you inscribed are lost.
Chaitra night, I sit alone,   once again, it becomes visible—
        among trees and branches, the illusion of your curved
            hand
in new-sprouted leaves   by some error they return   your
    old letters.

        The mallika blossom in tonight's forest
        is filled with fragrance—like your name.
Tender, the missive traced by your fingers   brought back to
    mind today
        some sorrow-filled script of parting.
On madhavi branches, dancing, dancing   your old
    handwriting.

1926

6

In order to find you anew, I lose you every moment
o beloved treasure.
        Because you wish to appear you become invisible
o beloved treasure.
Dearest, you aren't mine to hide, you're mine eternally—
        absorbed in time's playful momentary current
o beloved treasure.
When I seek you, my heart trembles with fear—
        I am rocked by a wave of love.

There's no end to you—so, becoming nothing, you put
   an end to yourself—
      that smile washes away my tears of separation
o beloved treasure.

1915

7

I'll let go of all pride
but your pride I'll hold dear.
The day I touch the dust on your feet
I'll summon, and tell, everyone.

Once your call makes its way to me
how will I keep it hidden, in secrecy?
Every action, every phrase
will become an expression of prayer.

On that day, whatever honours I've had
for whatever work, will grow distant from me.
Only your honour, in body and heart,
will resonate as melody.

The passer-by too will see as he passes
the news of you in the look on my face.
Under the window of all visible existence
I'll be sitting, abstractedly.

1901

Dream (Rabindranath Tagore)

       Far very far away
  in the kingdom of dreams, in Ujjain,
I can't recall when, I'd gone to look by the river Sipra
for my first love from a previous life.
Lodhra-pollen on her face, the lotus of creation
in her hands, kunda buds on the ears, kurubak blossoms
in her hair, body ensconced in blood-red cloth,
the anklets on her feet only half audible.
       One spring day
I'd painstakingly traced the long way back.

            In the interior of the Shiva temple then
         unfolded the sombre-sounding evening arati.
         The alleys with shops were empty, and from above
         streaks of evening light fell on dark buildings.

       My beloved's house
was on a narrow bent path, unfrequented, remote.
A conch-wheel imprinted on the door; on each side stood
two youthful kadamba trees, increasing liked adored sons.
  On the gate's white pillar
sat the solemn likeness of a lion.

            My beloved's doves had come back home,
            the peacock, deep in sleep, was perched on a golden
              staff.
            At this time, holding a clay lamp,
          gradually descended my Malabika.
She appeared beyond the doorway, above the stairs,
like the evening's Lakshmi, the evening star in her hands.
Her body's saffron scent and the incense in her hair

exhaled their ecstatic breath on all my body.
Given her red clothing had slipped slightly
the sandalwood pattern by her left breast was visible.
   Statue-like, she stood
in the stillness of an evening in which the town's humming
   had ceased.

                Noticing me, my love,
        slowly lowering her lamp by the door,
        came before me—taking my hand in hers,
        eyes kind, she softly asked only this:
        "O friend, I trust you're well?" Gazing on her face
        I started to speak, but had nothing to say.
        I'd forgotten that tongue. We thought hard and tried
        to summon each other's names, but they'd gone.
        So much we considered as we stared at each other,
        unstoppable tears falling from unblinking eyes!

So much we pondered beneath that door and tree!
   I don't know when and on what pretext
her soft hand arrived secretly in my right palm
like evening's bird reaching its nest. Her face
descended slowly on my chest
like a drooping lotus. Anxious, sorrowing,
my breath and hers, wordless, mingled together.

                The dark of night-time
        wholly obliterated Ujjain.
                The lamp by the door
        was put out at some point by an obstreperous breeze.
                In the Shiva temple near the banks of the Sipra
        the evening's arati came to an end.

                                    1897

Banalata Sen (Jibanananda Das)

For a thousand years I've been walking earth's paths,
from Sinhala's seas to the waters of Malaya in night's
    darkness
I've roamed over and over; in the grey world of Ashoka and
    Bimbisara
I was there; and, further, in the remote dark of Vidarbha city;
I'm a tired soul, the ocean of life foams around me;
I once had a few moments' peace from Natore's Banalata Sen.

Her hair the dimly remembered dark of Vidisha's night,
her face a carving from Shravasti; as, on an unending ocean,
the sailor whose boat's helm is broken, direction gone,
sees grass-green land within cinnamon islands,
so I caught sight of her in darkness; "Where were you all
    these days?"
raising her bird's-nest eyes, asked Natore's Banalata Sen.

At the end of the entire day, like the sound of dew,
evening comes; from its wings the hawk wipes off sunlight's
    smell;
as the world's colours go out the palimpsest arranges
the light of sparkling fireflies for a story;
all birds fly home—all rivers—life's commerce reaches an
    end;
only darkness remains, as I sit facing Banalata Sen.

1942

Notes

sandesh: A dry sweet, made in soft or hard varieties from a dairy product called chhana.

petha: A North Indian sweet made from the ash gourd. It's generally not eaten by Bengalis.

Creek Row: A lane used as a short cut between Upper Circular Road and College Street in Calcutta.

chhana: The cheese-like reduction of milk curd.

Rustom's: A Parsi restaurant in Delhi.

gajar mewa nu achar: A Parsi pickle made with carrots and raisins.

Adil: The poet Adil Jussawalla, who lives in Bombay.

kalbaisakhi: The brief showers that occur in Bengal in April and May, the hottest months of the year.

tapas: One of the meanings in Sanskrit has to do with meditation, asceticism, and spiritual practice.

From RAMANUJAN

Srinivasa Ramanujan (1887–1920): An Indian mathematician whose work came to the attention of the mathematician G. M. Hardy after Ramanujan wrote to him. Ramanujan was invited to Cambridge by Hardy and lived in England from 1914 to 1919. He then returned to India, where he lived until his death in 1920.

Papworth Hospital: Founded in 1918 as a sanatorium for discharged soldiers with tuberculosis. Ramanajan spent some time there after he was diagnosed with TB. It later became a centre for heart disease.

Srirangapatna: In Karnataka, it was the capital of Mysore under Tipu Sultan. It's where Tipu fell in a key battle to the British in 1799, with historic consequences for the empire.

Campus Kitchen: At the University of East Anglia.

"the Pleistocene Epoch itself / has come to an end": From J. H. Prynne's "The Glacial Question, Unsolved."

chalta: *Dillenia indica*, or the elephant apple.

ambal: A sweet-sour liquid dessert eaten after meals in the summer in Bengal.

tuchchho: Bengali for "insignificant" or "inconsequential."

teep: A Bengali word for bindi, or the dot Indian women sometimes put on their forehead.

"They": This poem is about the clay toys traditionally sold in markets in Calcutta: miniature replicas of vegetables like the patal, or padwal, or snake gourd. There were also small tin versions of kitchenware.

dhak: A drum played at different times of the day, starting early in the morning, during the harvest festival of the Pujas.

From ST CYRIL ROAD AND OTHER POEMS

"The world was all before them": From the closing lines of *Paradise Lost*, describing Adam and Eve's departure from paradise: "The World was all before them, where to choose / Thir place of rest, and Providence thir guide. / They, hand in hand, with wandring steps and slow, / Through *Eden* took their solitarie way."

Balthazar: The name of the donkey in Robert Bresson's 1966 film *Au Hasard Balthazar.*

Jata mat tata path: A Bengali adage attributed to the mystic Ramakrishna Paramhansa (1836–1886), meaning "There are as many paths [to God] as there are faiths."

DANTE ALIGHIERI THE NEW LIFE
Translated by Dante Gabriel Rossetti; Preface by Michael Palmer

ANTONELLA ANEDDA HISTORIAE
Translated by Patrizio Ceccagnoli and Susan Stewart

GUILLAUME APOLLINAIRE ZONE: SELECTED POEMS
Translated by Ron Padgett

AUSTERITY MEASURES THE NEW GREEK POETRY
Edited by Karen Van Dyck

SZILÁRD BORBÉLY BERLIN-HAMLET
Translated by Ottilie Mulzet

SZILÁRD BORBÉLY IN A BUCOLIC LAND
Translated by Ottilie Mulzet

ANDRÉ BRETON and PHILIPPE SOUPAULT THE MAGNETIC
FIELDS
Translated by Charlotte Mandel

MARGARET CAVENDISH *Edited by Michael Robbins*

NAJWAN DARWISH EXHAUSTED ON THE CROSS
Translated by Kareem James Abu-Zeid; Foreword by Raúl Zurita

NAJWAN DARWISH NOTHING MORE TO LOSE
Translated by Kareem James Abu-Zeid

BENJAMIN FONDANE CINEPOEMS AND OTHERS
Edited by Leonard Schwartz

GLORIA GERVITZ MIGRATIONS: POEM, 1976–2020
Translated by Mark Schafer

ZUZANNA GINCZANKA FIREBIRD
Translated by Alissa Valles

PERE GIMFERRER *Translated by Adrian Nathan West*

W. S. GRAHAM *Selected by Michael Hofmann*

SAKUTARŌ HAGIWARA CAT TOWN
Translated by Hiroaki Sato

MICHAEL HELLER TELESCOPE: SELECTED POEMS

MIGUEL HERNÁNDEZ *Selected and translated by Don Share*

RICHARD HOWARD RH ♥ HJ AND OTHER AMERICAN WRITERS
Introduction by Timothy Donnelly

RYSZARD KRYNICKI OUR LIFE GROWS
Translated by Alissa Valles; Introduction by Adam Michnik

LOUISE LABÉ LOVE SONNETS AND ELEGIES
Translated by Richard Sieburth

CLAIRE MALROUX DAYBREAK: NEW AND SELECTED POEMS
Translated by Marilyn Hacker

ARVIND KRISHNA MEHROTRA *Selected by Vidyan Ravinthiran;
Introduction by Amit Chaudhuri*

HENRI MICHAUX A CERTAIN PLUME
Translated by Richard Sieburth; Preface by Lawrence Durrell

MELISSA MONROE MEDUSA BEACH AND OTHER POEMS

JOAN MURRAY DRAFTS, FRAGMENTS, AND POEMS:
THE COMPLETE POETRY
*Edited and with an introduction by Farnoosh Fathi; Preface by
John Ashbery*

VIVEK NARAYANAN AFTER

EUGENE OSTASHEVSKY THE FEELING SONNETS

ELISE PARTRIDGE THE IF BORDERLANDS: COLLECTED POEMS

VASKO POPA *Selected and translated by Charles Simic*

J. H. PRYNNE THE WHITE STONES
Introduction by Peter Gizzi

ALICE PAALEN RAHON SHAPESHIFTER
Translated and with an introduction by Mary Ann Caws

A. K. RAMANUJAN THE INTERIOR LANDSCAPE: CLASSICAL
TAMIL LOVE POEMS

PIERRE REVERDY *Edited by Mary Ann Caws*

DENISE RILEY SAY SOMETHING BACK & TIME LIVED, WITHOUT
ITS FLOW

ARTHUR RIMBAUD THE DRUNKEN BOAT: SELECTED WRITINGS
*Edited, translated, and with an introduction and notes by Mark
Polizzotti*

JACK SPICER AFTER LORCA
Preface by Peter Gizzi

ALEXANDER VVEDENSKY AN INVITATION FOR ME TO THINK
Translated by Eugene Ostashevsky and Matvei Yankelevich

WANG YIN A SUMMER DAY IN THE COMPANY OF GHOSTS
Translated by Andrea Lingenfelter

WALT WHITMAN DRUM-TAPS: THE COMPLETE 1865 EDITION
Edited by Lawrence Kramer

NACHOEM M. WIJNBERG *Translated by David Colmer*

LAKDHAS WIKKRAMASINHA
Edited by Michael Ondaatje and Aparna Halpé

ELIZABETH WILLIS ALIVE: NEW AND SELECTED POEMS

RAÚL ZURITA INRI
Translated by William Rowe; Preface by Norma Cole